AFTER
AI

STRATEGIES *to*

SURVIVE
&THRIVE

ROOF MEDIA

A Roof Media release

After AI is a not-for-profit project.
Derek W Pearson asserts his right under
international copyright laws to be identified
as the author of this work, in part or in entirety.
Cover design and interior layout by Roof Media.
Efforts have been made to source only
copyright/ attribution-free images.
Please contact Roof Media
with queries.

ISBN: 978-0-473-45020-5
US English Edition

Visit the website:
www.afterai-project.com

mail to: roofmedianz@gmail.com

Contents

1

ARTIFICIAL

OR ORGANIC

Is Artificial Intelligence/ Automation a threat to our jobs and livelihoods?

The Wave

There's a gigantic wave of change, both terrible and wonderful, on the horizon. *Terrible*, because it'll bring about serious social and economic turmoil. And *wonderful*, because if we manage it well, it'll represent a huge step in our evolution as a species.

Artificial Intelligence – *AI* – is changing the world in ways that will hit each of us in our own individual space, head on, and we'll be forced to react in some way. Our ideas about work, society, freedom and individual expression will be jolted out of complacency and we'll have little choice but to act. We'll witness the biggest social upheaval in recent history, and the way we currently live and learn is not preparing us for it. Not even close.

In this book we'll look at strategies to manage the changes, and at new approaches to learning that'll keep ourselves and our children ahead of the AI curve.

A global appetite for comfort and leisure has ensured an enthusiastic reception for AI. We're happily anticipating a world where technology takes over menial tasks, and eliminates the mundane aspects of our lives.

Sounds pretty good so far... But we tend to forget that many of us earn a living doing menial – or at least *mundane* – work. And we're not thinking much about what will happen when that work no longer exists.

In just a few short decades, a lot of the work we do now will no longer be done by humans.

We aren't particularly worried about this – mostly, perhaps, because the huge scope of the situation is not yet clear to us – but everything we need to know about it is hiding right there in plain sight, like a *join-the-dots* puzzle that's too simplistic for us to bother with. We just need to take the time to bother a little – to join up those dots – and the picture will become clear.

The *popular* perception of AI is really only a fragment of a much bigger picture. The broader concept is less about technology, and more about a prevailing attitude:

Maximum comfort, for minimum effort.

It just happens that virtually *all* our comfort solutions are underpinned by AI-driven technology.

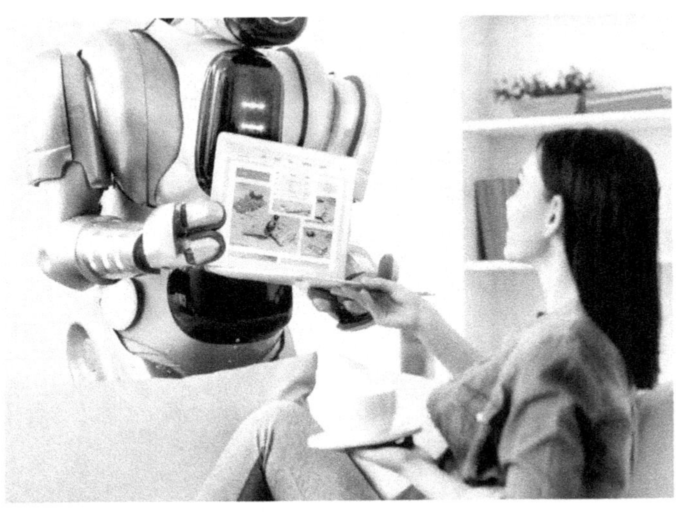

Surface aspects of AI are in plain sight everywhere we go. Perhaps we've ordered a meal by pushing buttons on a screen at a fast-food retailer, done our banking online, or bought our groceries at a self-checkout at the supermarket. This is just the shine on the surface of AI.

The following examples of recent AI/ automation are taken from a range of service industries. In each case, it's quite easy to imagine how the particular function will be expanded into a wider context.

A chain of convenience stores in China called *BingoBox* has introduced fully **AI-operated convenience stores** (automated checkouts; no human staff *at all,* apart from remote centralized security monitoring), and more look set to follow their example.[2]

At building sites, **robot brick-laying machines** are set to replace jobs on construction sites...[3]

... And with the arrival of *driverless cars, buses and trucks,*[4] the whole transport and delivery industries will change, requiring fewer and fewer human workers.[5]

Self-cleaning toilets are becoming a common sight in our cities.[6] The water-tight cubicle is programmed to lock itself between uses, then flush the entire facility with a high-pressure spray of disinfectant.

Perhaps *wait-staff* too will soon be out of a job: restaurants are starting to use a system where customers speak their orders into a device at their table, and a self-driving trolley rolls out with their food when it's ready.[7]

And white-collar workers won't be immune from the AI revolution either. Traditionally lucrative careers in accounting, law and medicine might always involve *some* human-to-human, front-line roles, but they also include a high degree of *diagnostic/ background* work, some of which can – and will – be automated.[8]

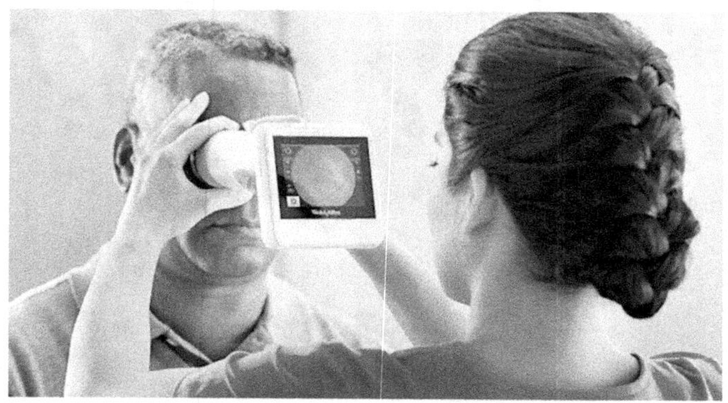

Early in 2018, the US Federal Drug Administration (FDA) approved a 100% AI-driven diagnostics system in the field of opthalmology (diseases and disorders of the eye), – which arguably opens the way to the wider field of medical diagnosis.[9] In the same way that using the internet, or channel surfing on a TV set doesn't require a degree in science, the few front-line staff required to operate AI-driven diagnostic technology will not require much training.

Indirect Job Displacement

Artificial Intelligence will displace jobs in two primary ways...

If the more obvious way is the *direct* taking-over of an existing job function, it makes sense to refer to the other way as *indirect*. Indirect job displacement by AI will come as a result of bigger-picture *paradigm shifts* caused by technological and sociological changes, and chief of these will be...

Online Business

In 2017, an estimated 1.66 billion people worldwide purchased goods online. During the same year, global e-retail sales amounted to 2.3 trillion U.S. dollars, and if the current trend continues – which seems likely – we'll see e-commerce command nearly *half* of the world's global retail market by 2038. [11]

AI underpins almost every aspect of what's become known as *e-commerce*, and is the driving force behind making the whole system as user-friendly as possible.[10] We won't have to wait long to witness its majestic proportions: a major migration of business across to e-commerce – in direct competition with traditional physical business – has already begun.

Real-World vs E-World

We like the experience of shopping at a real-world location, but price and convenience are becoming dominant factors in our everyday decisions. With intelligent interactive AI technology, the online market is constantly introducing new and better ways to **simulate** the experience of **real-world shopping**, and as a result, more and more customers are choosing the online option, rather than pay higher prices at a physical store.

One day soon, a handful of giant online mega-stores that sell anything and everything cheaply and deliver fast, will dominate the international retail industry. This is very bad news for real-world, physical businesses, who – with their high overhead costs – won't be able to compete with their online competitors.

A Brighter Future

Yes. There are some big challenges on the horizon, but it's not all bad. Technology will, in the end, serve us well. It'll help clean up the planet,[17] economically stream-line our lifestyle, push us to discover more of ourselves, and ultimately bring us all closer together.

But how can we be sure we'll have the guts and the wisdom and the generosity to get us through this junction?

Because we humans meet a challenge when we absolutely have to. When our backs are truly against the wall, we start figuring out ways to make things work — especially if it's obvious we can't avoid the issue!

2

SUPERFICIAL

OR PROFOUND

Is what we **appear to be** more important than **what we are?**

Evidence

"There's more to intelligence than meets the eye..."

... Trite observation? Perhaps. Pertinent? Definitely: grasping just how much we *don't* know about intelligence will be a critical issue in the coming years.

Our perceptions of both artificial and human intelligence are strongly influenced by *superficial evidence,* and we need to reconsider this before we can adequately prepare for our future.

The Duck Test

However clever modern science has become, it can't yet quantify the human mind. And it's important we look squarely at this stark truth, because it's impossible for any of us – no matter what level of authority or expertise – to get the measure of something we don't fully understand. *The evidence we seek and gather will always mirror our limited perceptions.*

The subject of the wartime bio-pic *Imitation Game* (2014, Black Bear Pictures), *Alan Turing* was one of the fathers of modern Artificial Intelligence.

In 1950, Turing developed what would become known as the "Turing Test". Test evaluators would observe, on a screen, a text-only conversation between two test subjects – one of which was human, the other, artificial. If evaluators couldn't tell which was which, the AI subject would pass the test: it was *intelligent*.

The Turing test is still considered by some to be a relevant scientific test today. But it's essentially a "duck test": *"if it* looks *like a duck,* swims *like a duck, and* quacks *like a duck, then it must* be... *a duck"*.

Turing himself was aware that intelligence was too profound a concept to measure in a superficial way. But that didn't stop him formulating a test that ignored the vast underlying landscape of consciousness and perception that underpins human intelligence.

Is it logical to ignore part of an equation when it could effect the end result? While we can't currently quantify the subjective, inner-world properties of the mind – such as curiosity, creativity and imagination – *we know they're there.* Whether or not we can measure them in concrete terms, they figure large in the fabric of intelligence!

The Subjective Realm

Often it's a comfort to us that no one can hear what we're thinking. A *relief,* even. Our thoughts run unchallenged and free in an internal world that's completely invisible to others.

Let's call this private world of consciousness the *Subjective Realm.* It's a view from the inside looking out; a first-person perspective of the world through our own unique set of filters.

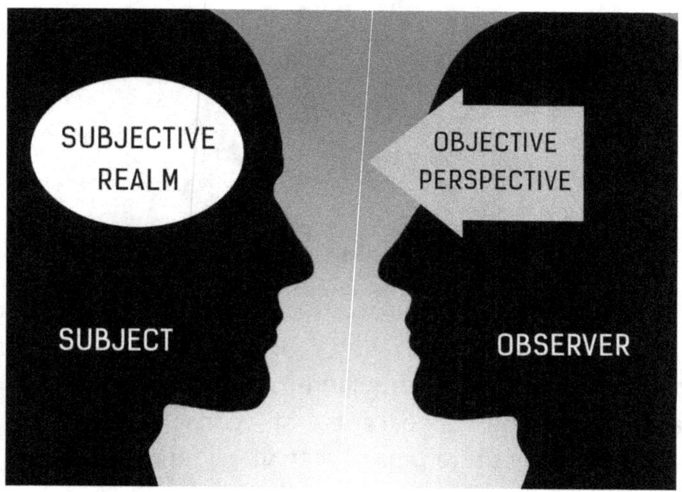

We have no meaningful way of measuring this realm, but we still try! We evaluate it in a purely *objective* (observational) way – from the *outside* looking *in* – and tend to see only what fits into a "useful" context in the outer world.

Properties that can't be measured using standard units such as inches, seconds, kilowatts or degrees, are a mystery to us. They won't fit into a practical context, so we tend to be dismissive of them. It's a blinkered way of looking at things, but we've managed to get this far without serious damage. Mostly.

But if we keep the blinkers on, we're going to start bumping into things very soon. And hurting ourselves. Those unquantifiable properties that we've largely ignored for so long, are going to be the only things standing between us and redundancy by automation.

The fact is, everything that is calculable now – in those terms of inches, seconds, kilowatts, degrees, etc – is going to be fair game for automation, because calculation is a computer's number-one strength!

Defining Intelligence

Starting in 1956, Artificial Intelligence enjoyed a "summer" period of very generous state funding in western countries, because scientists had claimed they could replicate human intelligence within a decade. But by 1973, it was clear they were nowhere near their goal, and the money-faucet was turned off.

So, *how could the experts get it so wrong...?* They were defining intelligence as something scarcely more than complex calculations. They mistook the limited evidence they were able to gather, for something approaching a complete understanding of the human mind.

A pocket calculator far outperforms most humans' ability to do sums in our heads — but does that mean the calculator is "smarter"...?

... Only in a *very narrow way,* right? Modern AI might be much more powerful than the simple calculator, but no matter how amazing its abilities to assess, cross-reference, spontaneously learn and 'think for itself', AI will always be limited by the **kinds of data** available to it.

A human's broad-ranging 'smarts' are based on the organic sum of a lifetime of *experiential* data; everything we've ever seen, heard, felt, dreamed, touched, loved, hated, envied... the smell of apples that time we fell off our bicycle; the fear of falling from the tree we climbed, combined with the exhilaration of achievement... etcetera, etcetera. Countless stimuli. Countless cross-associations.

And the very nature of our logic makes things even more complex: human logic is imperfect. *Convenient thinking* is a fundamental characteristic of the human mind. To a substantial degree, it's our messy logic; our willingness to be foolish, that defines our organic intellectual nature. ***Our humanness.***

The logic that underpins our thinking is shot through with contradictions and inconsistencies, and we all have some degree of inability – or *reluctance* – to step up and make those mental connections that would arguably be the cleanest, healthiest and most honest.

Could AI understand, for example, such illogical practices as smoking, drinking, drugs or over-eating, when the impact on underlying health and wellbeing was negative? Or even the most innocent pleasures like bungee-jumping, sex or jogging, that nonetheless carry risk, or at least a rush triggered by fear, or physical damage?

None of these contradictions would make logical sense to a machine, because *there is no in-between state of logic in an artificial mind.*

AI either *knows,* or it *does not know:* A one, or a zero.

What we humans manage to achieve through this mess of multiple-layer logical contradictions is truly wonderful. We make great logical leaps. We *imagine.* We *create.* All because of the flexible, untethered nature of our logic. But if we purposefully set about reproducing this in non-organic artificial intelligence, the result would *not* be wonderful. The best we could hope for would be a deliberately deceptive AI mind. A *lying robot.* The worst: a truly dangerous monster!

But before we panic, we should remember this: the multitude of doomsday-robot movies we've seen are not very realistic. It's unlikely anyone will deliberately make something they know will be deceitful. An unpredictable "loose-cannon" like this would *predictably* pose as much risk to its manufacturer as it would anyone else!

Unique Minds

Albert Einstein, Marie Curie and Lewis Carroll are part of a long list of historical luminaries now believed to have had the condition known as *Asperger's Syndrome*. All three displayed abilities that were so extraordinary, that their lack of "normal" skills was overlooked.

Einstein, Curie and Carroll all had an unusually intense focus on their subjects of interest, and they were remarkable people who were hard not to notice! But what about the multitudes of *less*-remarkable people – then, and now – whose particular strengths and focuses go unrecognized and unexpressed, because we're not looking specifically for them?

Our learning systems are at last beginning to recognize the *concept* of an individual's uniqueness and its rich potential, but we still demand the *same evidence*, of the *same abilities* from each "unique" student.

If we're cold-bloodedly *practical* about this, it's an issue of the greater group missing out on the huge untapped potential of its individuals. On the other hand, if we're warm-bloodedly *humane* about it, the issue lies more in the suffering of the individual, who faces a daily struggle to be something they're not.

The Resumé Culture

The resumé. It's our ticket to a successful future. To *employment. Financial security. Comfort. Social function.*

There's a lot of pressure to build a strong resumé. So much so, that we tend to define our lives to a substantial degree by what looks good on our CV. What will **sell** us.

An unfortunate aspect of competitive 21st century life, is the increasing pressure on our learning systems to make their graduates as "qualified" and as "employable" as possible.

Learning becomes *less* about understanding ourselves and the world we live in; *more* about getting good grades and packaging ourselves for the employment market. The end-goal becomes the fulcrum that everything else pivots on, and there's less and less stopping to smell the roses on the way.

This makes us very **evidence-focused** – often to the extent that we sideline things that don't boost our personal saleability in some tangible way. But where does that leave abilities that we *can't* measure or assess objectively...?

The first step is to *define* those abilities – measurable or not – that are imperative to our future...

The **CiCi** Imperatives

- Curiosity

- Imagination

- Creativity

- Initiative

Can't be taught; existing ability must be actively developed upon

Curiosity. Imagination. Creativity. Initiative. The four *CiCi Imperatives* are basic necessities for our future survival: they represent a sea-wall against the tide of automation.

"C" for Curiosity

The first "C" in CiCi is *Curiosity.* This might be the hardest property of all to get an intellectual handle on, because it leaves no obvious footprint in the visible world. We can't measure it, but it's certainly there. And keeping sight of it is much more important than we think.

We're pretty much resigned to the idea that the gradual fading of our childhood curiosity and enthusiasm is just a natural part of growing up... *But is it really?*

What if we're unwittingly suppressing this important attribute in our children? Pushing their curiosity down, down; continually telling it, *not now. Be quiet.* Causing it to shrivel and retract and eventually shut up...?

We don't want that – now, less than ever, because *curiosity will be our single greatest asset in a post-AI context*. But some of our traditional ideas about a child's place in the world, and about the ways they should learn, afford little room for a child's persistent questioning.

Curiosity opens the mind and makes us receptive. It's the fertile soil from which organic intelligence grows; the *foundation stone of all that differentiates humans from machines.*

Imagination, creativity and *initiative* all spring from a healthy curiosity.

"I" for Imagination

Imagination is the courage to reach *beyond the known,* and into the world of *what-if;* to take new and untested threads of ideas and tie them experimentally together.

Imagination allows us to grasp possibilities and potentials; to mentally step outward and stand in a different place; to consider an alternative perspective.

To be broad-minded,

compassionate...

and *creative.*

"C" for Creativity

Creativity is mistakenly thought to be the preserve of arty types – painters, writers, sculptors, musicians – who are mostly doomed to a life of poverty.

The fact is, *each and every one of us is naturally creative in our own way,* but our current learning methods cramp our notion of creativity into a prescribed frame.

Traditionally, we try to bring discipline and order to a child's mind as early as possible. This is a genuine attempt to develop healthy, functional thinking while the child is still "impressionable", but it's at least partially to blame for our disconnection with a very valuable aspect of our intelligence.

Ordered thinking has its place, but then so does random, undisciplined thinking. Random-mind is the **_very source of creativity._**

Every child starts out with a healthy level of randomness, and therefore easy access to their own particular flavor of creative thinking. At some point, the child can be supported in bringing order to their thinking, but this shouldn't happen before they're ready for it. When we force discipline on a child's mind, we squash their random thinking, and as a consequence, their creativity.

It's best that a child is allowed to first *establish a relationship* with randomness, and to then arrive at discipline in their own way, and in their own time. This will come naturally when – through an activity they find exciting – they eventually feel motivated to find the mental order that allows them to achieve their goals.

This "mental order" may not be what we recognize today as disciplined thinking, and it might not happen as early as we'd currently think appropriate. But we can't realistically impose a standard expectation on uniqueness without damaging it! Each of us has our *own flavor* of intelligence, and our *own flavor* of creativity that should neither be dictated nor scheduled.

When we arrive at ordered thinking in our own time, we establish a choice of channels to think through. Order, or randomness; randomness or order. Either of which we can use when appropriate, and to our best advantage.

"I" for Initiative

Initiative is probably the easiest to grasp of the CiCi Imperatives, because we've valued the concept since before workplace automation was an issue. But the changing context requires a deeper notion of initiative.

We have to ask ourselves, *where* does our initiative come from? What is initiative's ***initializing spark?***

We've always been satisfied for that spark to come from any motivating source. But to achieve the real-McCoy version of initiative, the source must come from within; from the subjective realm. This can only be achieved if we work to preserve the most useful property our children have... Their ***curiosity.***

... How, then, do we achieve ***that?***

3

PASSIVE

OR ACTIVE

What makes us **more than machines?**

Removing the Bar

Far more important than *what* we know, is *how* we know. The ability to use our minds well needs to take precedence over what we store in there: computers will *always* beat us at that game!

We've been consciously raising the bar in our learning systems for decades now. To *make our kids smarter.* To *keep up with the wider ground-swell in knowledge.* More specifically, though: we've done it to keep ourselves and our kids above the employability threshold. Food on table. Roof over heads.

But continuing to operate within this increasingly frantic upward spiral might have the opposite effect to what we're intending: it could actually make us *less* employable in the coming years.

Focusing our kids on *results, results, results,* makes their learning all about **ticking the right boxes.** The problem with this is two-fold:

1) Their qualifications will show only that they've satisfied set criteria. AI automates according to "set criteria" very well, and when employers need better reasons to hire a live human employee over a cheaper AI option, the ability to self-motivate/ perform *beyond* set boundaries will increasingly be a factor.

2) Perhaps more importantly, the fixed results focus itself will have narrowed the learner's *basic concept* of learning – impacting negatively on their actual *ability* to operate outside the box, and beyond the scope of AI...

... If raising the bar higher and higher isn't the answer, perhaps we have to remove the bar from the equation!

A Horse Named Curiosity

The child is full of questions: *Why...? When...? How...?* But is asked to sit quietly and listen while a professional grown-up tells them all the answers they're supposedly going to need some time in their future.

Answers, answers, answers...

This is how our current learning methods work. Answers all day, every day, for at least ten years of schooling. Answers before questions... ***Cart before horse.***

Learning in a context where *question* is given such a low priority, it's really no wonder a child's curiosity fades.

Like the horse, curiosity's proper place is out front, leading the way. Providing ***forward propulsion***. Curiosity brings forth *questions*, which in turn invite *answers*. This is a natural, self-initiating sequence that empowers a child to engage with their world, and to be an initiating aspect of it.

Curiosity is a fundamental driving force that motivates us. It can't be taught, or instilled or scheduled. *What is already there* must be nurtured and allowed to grow at its own pace, and in its own fashion.

The Passive Learner

Fancy stuff aside, we need now – more than ever – to be *self-motivating.* We can no longer afford to sit on our butts and wait for someone to tell us what to do, when to do it, and how to do it – but that means we're in trouble, because the way we currently learn *encourages* serious butt-parking.

Traditional thinking insists a child takes a ***passive*** role in their learning. Because kids supposedly can't judge for themselves what they do, and don't need to know, they're placed at the blunt end of the whole learning process. Their learning is *brought to them.*

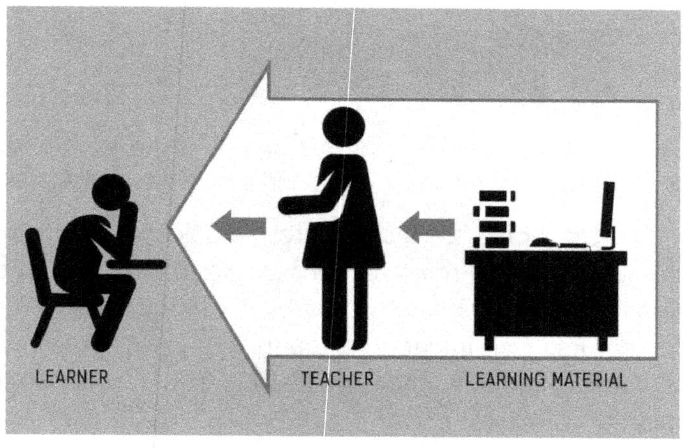

The presumption that wiser, older people need to tell children *what, how* and *when* to learn is so ingrained, and so taken-as-read, that we don't think to question its accuracy. But can we realistically expect a young person to finish ten-plus years of learning in a passive context, and then go out into today's world as a self-motivating individual?

If self-motivation can't be taught, where does it come from, and how is it developed? First up, we have to feel we have a true, meaningful stake in our learning. Even as small children, we need to be supported in feeling *personally responsible* for it from the very beginning.

Responsibility is not just an outward behavior. It's first and foremost an *inward ownership* of our own choices and their consequences that *might then* manifest itself in outward behavior. The way to support the growth of true, inner responsibility is to *afford* responsibility. Initiative grows from a sense of *being an initializer* in our lives.

The Active Learner

As much as possible, the learner needs to be afforded responsibility for what, how and when they learn: ***the learner must become the active party in their learning.***

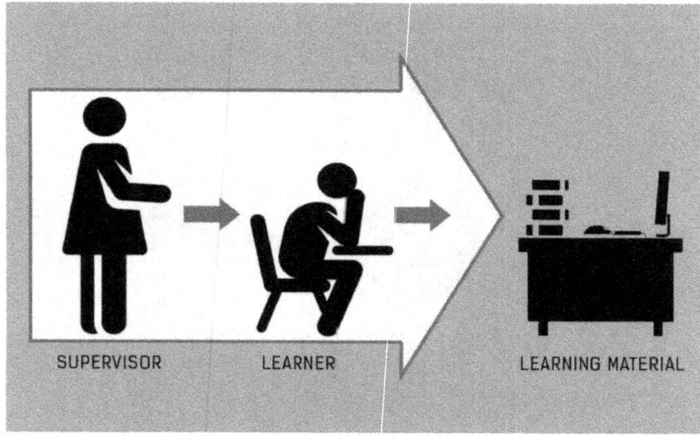

Active Learning is self-directed – in other words, the child is the driver of their own learning. But it's important to recognize that *self-directed* does not mean *left to one's own devices*. Supervision and consultation are key factors, because the child still needs some shape to their learning, and when appropriate, the benefit of other people's experience. They'll consult with a supervisor, but every effort should be made to allow the child to decide, up front, what's to be achieved during their day, and when.

The child is more likely to respond to a framework they themselves have put in place; all the more so if they know they can adjust the framework the following day.

Managing Individualized Learning

Current learning systems assume a conveniently broad overlap between one child's needs and another's. But every single child is unique, which means every single child's *learning needs* are unique too. If our aim – at the very least – is to establish an advantage over AI in the job market, we need to fully recognize human uniqueness in our learning systems, because this is where our real strengths lie.

One of the great sticking-points with regards to an increased focus on the individual child, is the belief that it necessitates more teaching staff. For sure: if we imposed this requirement on the current *passive* learning system, we'd *absolutely* have that problem! But a change of fundamental methods from passive to *active*, should see the child take an increased share of responsibility, and keep the supervisory burden manageable.

A Two-Layer Cake

Standardization is unavoidable when using a set curriculum – but set standards can't address individual learning needs... This is a potential stalemate if we want to preserve a qualification system.

If, however, we split our learning into two distinct layers, we can have our cake, and eat it too. While *Layer One* would be a foundational learning environment *without* set curricula or testing, *Layer Two* would preserve the standardization required for specialist qualification. Learners would be able to move from one stream to the other when individually appropriate.

Non-Curricular Active Learning (NCAL) would phase in to replace the current elementary/ primary school system. The most important time to allow for a child's unique learning needs is right at the outset – they need the time and the resources to establish their own own learning style, and to come to grips with what it is they're curious about in the world. For this reason, the entry into structured learning needs to be fluid in terms of learning objectives and learning material. Any form of standardization, including set curricula and testing, will nullify the aim of an individual learning focus.

Layer Two (Curricular Active Learning) would offer material similar to current high schools in terms of standardized curricula and testing, but would retain from the foundation layer (NCAL) the very distinct emphasis on *active* learning methods.

Layer Two should be an option, rather than a fait-accompli. Each child should have complete freedom to choose when – and even *if* – they make the move into the curricular spectrum, where they specialize and gain qualifications in one or more subjects. Rather than obliging the learner to study subjects they're not interested in, the existing qualification system would be altered to allow for single-subject qualification. The learner might also divide their time between CAL and NCAL depending on their needs – it may be appropriate to have a dual campus in each school, offering both CAL and NCAL services separately, but close together for the sake of convenience.

Personal Project-Based Study

Layer-one NCAL learning activity would be project-based: a continuing series of modular studies, of subjects that take the child's interest at the time – no rules or guidelines concerning "usefulness" or "appropriateness" should be laid (apart from a fundamentally healthy focus); the fact that the subject generates curiosity in the learner is reason enough.

Supervisory staff will consult with the learner to establish there's a plan in place, then take a step back to allow things to happen. They'll then be involved periodically and when needed. Children can also schedule time to help one another, regardless of age and experience; their opinions should always be heard.

Objectives will be mapped out by the child with supervisory help. As small children they can be subtly steered towards reading – using storytelling and games where possible – but no standardized learning objectives should be applied, nor pressure to learn to read or write by any particular age. Use of text-to-speech/ speech-to-text software can facilitate access to information and help construct their projects, until they themselves grow curious (or frustrated!) about what they're missing out on. Support needs will vary, so flexible streaming will be necessary to keep things manageable.

The size and scope of projects would be decided by

the child, and most research/ compiling/ printing of materials done on a computer. Presentation of the project should preferably involve expressive activities such as drawing, model making, music, or verbal explanation to the group. Children might also be encouraged to include activities that involve further learning, like simple math: for example, drawing up a budget for a parent-supported field trip, or comparing data they discover about their chosen subject.

Competition and comparison will have no place in this new context. The child's individual needs, and the nature of each project, will dictate the pace and relevance of their learning.

Deeper technical learning (spelling, grammar, punctuation, advanced math), should be encouraged only as a means to support the child's *current project,* and only as far as the child requires; no further, unless the child is specifically interested.

Blurred Lines

Play in Learning

Play is a crucial element in a child's healthy development, for many reasons, including a beneficial influence in their learning. It stimulates imagination and improves interpersonal skills.

If it's motivated by curiosity, learning will become less distinguishable from play, and from work. The lines between each should blur; perhaps even disappear. Until now we've been inclined to think of the three activities as three different areas of life, that should be separated and scheduled to protect the integrity of each. This is going to have to change, or at least relax to some considerable degree. Learning should be a twenty-four-hour, seven-day-a-week, ***life-long occupation.***

As recently as two generations ago, children happily took themselves off to play in forests, parks, streams and tumble-down houses, and they did this without a whiff of concern from their parents. This had a hugely beneficial effect on a child's development and general sense of well-being. Today, because of an increased awareness of safety issues, we can't realistically allow so much unmonitored activity, but we can provide practical support that allows our kids regular freedom to explore in safety.

A child can be taken regularly to new, unfamiliar environments, and encouraged to explore – sometimes alone; sometimes with others. Different skills are gained from each, and so both are important. If they get wet or dirty, *so much the better!* We can cheerfully hand them the means to clean themselves and their clothes...

... Or not ☺

We should also keep in mind that play and exploration is something to be done *for its own sake*, and not necessarily with specific goals or strategies attached!

Broad Horizons

"... Because I say so" might get things done quickly, but it's an attitude that crushes initiative and promotes passivity. It gives the message, *"trust me, I know better than you do"*, which paves the way for the child to grow up with a tendency to trust in a higher authority; someone who "knows better than they do"... Not at all helpful in developing independent thinking!

If we want our children to move forward and embrace greater things – to *at the very least* be functional in an automated world – we need to encourage them always to think and reason for themselves. Even if it seems inconvenient. Likewise, a parent's wholesale drive to instill their own *right and wrong* values in their child encourages a narrow, black and white view. The child adopts the parent's values, not because they've thought them through and arrived at the same conclusion, but because they've been told *that's how it is.*

It's vitally important that the child is *regularly exposed to differing points of view* on any single situation or event, because this awakens a *depth* of thinking; an ability to imagine alternative possibilities to the familiar status quo.

Visits to foreign cultures – especially those with another language – are extremely mind-broadening. Choosing one specific destination, and spending time communicating and negotiating one's way around, is infinitely more enriching than a tourist's fleeting impression of multiple destinations.

But even in a home country, it's beneficial to cultivate relations with children and families from *other cultures and values* systems, and regularly encounter movies, music and stories that show contrasting ideas and lifestyles.

The Driver

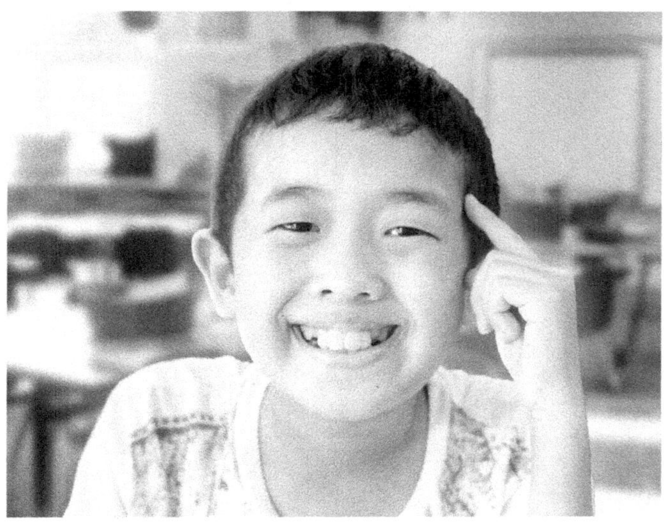

The desire to discover more should be the primary driving factor in everything a child learns. A good supervisor will be on the lookout for opportunities to encourage the development of skills that help that discovery to happen.

NCAL will serve as an effective learning foundation because the child – in their excitement to satisfy their curiosity – will be motivated to learn the broad range of skills that enables them to research and collect their material, and to communicate their findings. Literacy and numeracy will be necessary tools to access and understand what excites them about the world, and their abilities will flourish with the accomplishment of each project, beyond childhood and throughout the rest of their lives...

...Yes: *throughout the rest of their lives.* Why stop? Their curiosity will guide them on to learn more widely and deeply because they've learned *how* to drive their own learning in a healthy way.

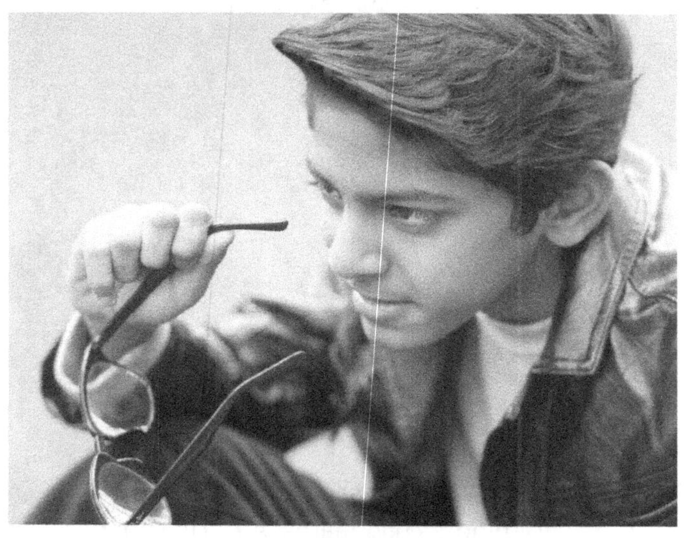

NCAL represents a radical change - this in itself will be a sticking point for a lot of people. But let's be clear about this: *the world itself is going to be radically changed by Artificial Intelligence.* If we don't act in some radical way to meet this change, we'll find ourselves in serious trouble.

Perhaps other, adequately radical answers lie elsewhere. If that's the case, we need to *look* elsewhere and come up with solid solutions...

... and we need to do it soon!

4

FULFILLMENT

OR SURVIVAL

What **motivates** us to **work?**

Occupation

A few short decades ago there was a struggle to gain social recognition for the role of "home-maker" as a bona-fide occupation, because we had this thing about what constituted a "real job". It was tricky to re-define the concept back then, and quite soon it's going to be *very* tricky to smack that definition into a whole new ballpark.

... But that's certainly what we're going to have to do. Our occupation is whatever it is we do with our days. It could be a paid job like baker, veterinary surgeon or accountant; could be a non-paid job like softball coach or business mentor. Could be something as "non-productive" (in conventional terms) as sitting and contemplating: there are times when that's necessary!

Re-skilling

The Ceiling

If we could re-train all our displaced workers for jobs above AI's capability ceiling, re-skilling might be a good option. But our problem is that individual human workers *themselves* have a capability ceiling – and one that's perhaps less flexible than their AI competition.

The initiative, creativity and subtle judgment-calls that are beyond AI capabilities, will be beyond many humans too – and if they *are* capable and take the substantial step of retraining, how will they fare in a competitive market already chock-full of passionately-driven people who deliberately chose those jobs?

Voiced loudly in various reports about the future of work, are confident claims that AI will generate a whole raft of new jobs.[22] New types of jobs will certainly be created by the proliferation of AI, but the huge *numbers* of new jobs forecast are calculated using yesterday's statistical models: no longer relevant today, and even less so in the case of future projections. Then there's the problem of suitability. Data analysis, software development and social media specialization are quoted as the big growth areas. The majority of new jobs quoted are almost exclusively within the technology sector: not everyone's thing, and not much help to people in the majority of the work spectrum.

Microsoft's Bill Gates recently suggested we redeploy a substantial number of our AI-displaced workers into care-giving, because it happens to be a growth industry. Care work for the elderly, mentally ill, physically disabled or infirm requires a special kind of temperament[15] – *patience; compassion; stamina; generosity; integrity.* Few of us have the right combination of character traits, and those who do aren't necessarily interested in this kind of work. It's certainly preferable that people doing this job have their hearts in it, and that they do it well!

The issue highlights our tendency to think in terms of a "labor pool". As if workers should be capable of any job they're pointed at; a one-size-fits-all cog that will work in any machine.

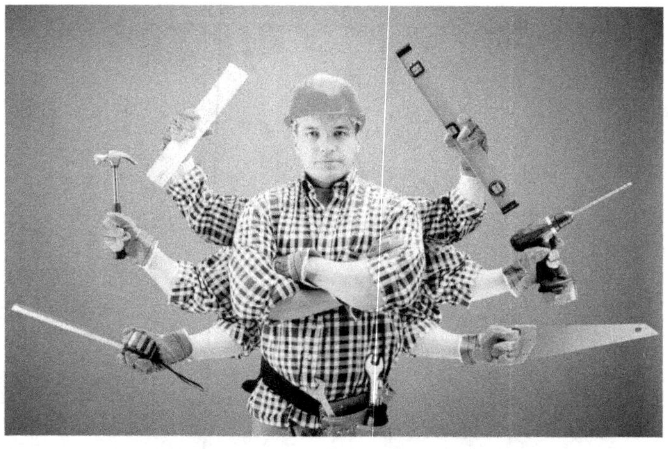

It's a job…! Why can't we just knuckle down and do it…?

Each of us is smart in different ways, and our own particular smarts make us suitable for work in some fields, but not in others. We've known this for ages, but it doesn't seem to filter into our idea of practical reality.

But beyond the practicalities lies a deeper, more fundamental reason *not* to shoe-horn people into jobs…

A New Kind of Wealth

Which is the primary motivator in our choice of work? Fulfillment or survival...? And what does this say about our lives?

Being "poor" can be miserable, but perhaps the most crippling form of poverty is poverty of the heart. All the money and pretty things in the world can't bring fulfillment to someone who is poor of heart.

A lot of us believe we can live *without* genuine fulfillment. Our forefathers were so convinced that it was an impossible dream, that they started talking us out of fulfillment from an early age, rather than allow us to grow up into disillusionment. As they told it, we *work, we eat, we sleep, we party a bit and we die*. We believed them. And we're still actively maintaining the self-fulfilling prophecy today.

A passive education strips us of the ability to *decide*

for ourselves what constitutes fulfillment, and instead reinforces a prescribed notion of what *should* be fulfilling. We're constantly hauled off our own track of curiosity and placed firmly back on the main trunk line: the track that leads to a one-size-fits-all "successful life", and we're "corrected" enough times that it sticks. But if and when we do actually "arrive", we don't feel fulfilled...

Is that really any surprise?

There's a saying that goes: *hope for the best; plan for the worst.*

Some would say this is a realist's view of the world – others would call it cynical or perhaps old-fashioned – but it's very much a part of our thinking today. It's how we generally relate to our work choices. Our choice *whether* to work in a conventional job, and *what type* of work we'll do, is first and foremost driven by survival – and as a secondary consideration, we *hope* for a measure of fulfillment along the way.

It's essential that we change these priorities. A work choice motivated by survival is usually a choice to be a small cog in a larger wheel, and therefore a choice to be *very replaceable* in the future. Cog-in-the-wheel type jobs will be among the first to be replaced: either by AI technology, or by another human who's more self-determined... or maybe just cheaper!

Work that's rewarding involves levels of subtle reasoning and creativity that are far less likely to be within the capabilities of AI. A choice for fulfillment is a win-win strategy: You get to do something you like, and at the same time stay above the AI ceiling.

The AI/ automation issue is lighting a fire under our tails. It's going to force our hand and drive us to make tough decisions that perhaps go against much of what we've been taught...

It's going to take some courage to get through this, especially in the early stages, when we'll be sorely tempted to stick to what we know. But it's also going to force us onto a much more self-determining track. It'll make us stronger individuals, with the self-afforded freedom to express our genuine selves. And it'll ultimately re-align us with true wealth: the ability to embrace fulfillment.

A fulfilling life is certainly a heartwarming concept. But in practical terms, how is this realistic? We have visions of a cheaper future with AI/ automation, but we still have to eat and keep a roof over our heads. If an activity we find fulfilling is not profitable, how do we *live...*?

The UBI:

Zuckerberg　　　　Gates　　　　Musk

Money for Nothing?

Technology magnates Mark Zuckerberg (Facebook), Bill Gates (Microsoft) and Elon Musk (PayPal; Tesla) are in favor of a UBI — or at least see it as a measure that'll be inevitable in the future.

A state that embraces a Universal Basic Income system pays all of its citizens a set, regular income reflecting minimum living costs, regardless of their financial position.

Even in highly competitive societies like the USA, the UBI concept is slowly gaining popularity. In a 2018 Gallup and Northeastern University poll, 48 percent of Americans agreed that a universal income program is a positive solution.[23]

Concerns

Negatives regarding a UBI system include concerns about "money for nothing" – some societies have a fundamental belief that a UBI would promote laziness. Others think that having our fundamental needs met takes the focus away from mere survival, and gives us the best platform from which to achieve.

A major sticking point is where the money needed to pay the UBI would come from. Most respondents in the US poll were against personal income tax increases funding the UBI. They preferred taxing companies who profit from AI and autonomous technologies in general: the businesses that effectively cause AI job displacement.

A tax might be best formulated by industry-type, on a multi-tier basis; according to the level of influence (direct and indirect) each has on job displacement, from a specified date onwards. Setting an "influence" start date is important, because automation has already been causing moderately significant job displacement for over half a century (factory robots come to mind). We'd need to nail down exactly which types of technology-use should be taxed, and from when.

But even for a relatively small country, the cost of providing a UBI would run to many billions of dollars per year: would an AI/ Automation tax cover this? It's hard to say for sure, but big tech companies are among the highest earners in world business (Apple's net profit for 2016 was US$45.69 billion, and Amazon's was US$177.87 billion, to name a few), and even a small percentage of their action would constitute a fair slice of the UBI bill.

And coming paradigm shifts could further enhance the size of that slice. Oil has been a cornerstone of the world's economy for many years, but this is set to change over the next few decades. While the west makes slow but steady progress in the development of electric cars, China has been quietly building its own very substantial EV industry.[24]

In an effort to improve living and environmental conditions, China's billion-plus population will soon be incentivized into buying electric cars like the *Nio* (pictured above). The flow-on effect from this is likely to hit the rest of the world soon after, squeezing the value of oil, and introducing cheap, high-quality electric cars into the international market. Big technological paradigm shifts like this will certainly cause job displacement, but on the positive side, they'll also help us target industries that should contribute to a UBI.

In any case, if the profitability of technology-based big business comes at the expense of people's livelihoods, then taxing those profits to help pay for a UBI appears to make sense. That said; if that's the direction we choose, it's our responsibility to make sure that a UBI-supported lifestyle has the best chance to be productive.

The way we *learn* is an essential component in this issue. If a Universal Basic Income is implemented *in tandem* with an active learning system, our future generations will have a better platform from which to grow up more self-motivating and therefore, more productive.

A New Start

Life with a UBI

Assuming we *do* adopt a UBI system, a new lifestyle with basic everyday needs taken care of might not turn out to be the life of ease some of us had hoped for. It'll be up to us individually to build upon the supportive foundation the UBI provides, and not all of us will be motivated to pro-actively achieve this.

The UBI won't cover extras like entertainment and treats. For those of us whose work options are limited by AI job displacement, we'll have food on the table and a roof over our heads, but our lives will be simpler and might lack the luxuries we've taken for granted in the past.

The primary issue here is not material wealth – or the lack of it – but *meaningful activity:* we need to be doing something with our days that we personally find meaningful. This affords a deeper, more fulfilling quality of life that material luxuries can't touch.

5

COMPETITION

OR CO-OPERATION

Is it **selfish** to be
who we really are?

Us or Them

Our fundamental needs are quite simple. Food. Shelter. Love. Fulfillment. It's the same for all of us. Whatever our individual picture of an ideal world looks like, at the very least it needs to start with these things.

Currently we think it's normal – even healthy – to *compete* for our fundamental needs. And we compete at every level, especially when it comes to making a living.

But the gentle live-and-let-live days of competition have gone. The stakes have gone way up in education, home-buying, social credibility; in employment and in the economic arena as a whole.

Increasingly, businesses have to use drastic measures – like cutting staff, sourcing cheaper overseas product – if not *intentionally* to put their competitors out of business, to at least avoid going bust themselves.

Nevertheless, many *do* go out of business. Every day. The competitive corridor is wedge-shaped; ever-narrowing, and we've moved so far along that corridor that fewer and fewer can squeeze through it together. It's *them* versus *us*, and we invariably choose *us*.

But do other political systems have the answers? Survivors of failed communist regimes tell of living a daily lie. Of great hardship, made worse by a desperate pressure to pretend that everything was just fine. To be seen to be thankful and joyously happy with what the proletariat was providing for them, despite a terrible lack of basic needs like food, warmth and freedom of self-expression.

Of course, the people running the communist regimes were generally fairly low on integrity, but at the grass-roots level, there was also a lack of real *responsibility* and *generosity* in the hearts of the citizens. Then again, is that any surprise? Not a single nation in the world can claim such fine attributes in a majority of their populace.

Imposing a system of sharing on unmotivated, self-centered people is never going to work.

Despite popular notions, we humans are not born selfish. The selfishness that grows in us comes primarily from a lack-mentality; for the most part caused by the traditional beliefs that *lack motivates* us, and *fulfillment makes us lazy*. We're forever holding fulfillment out in front of ourselves, like the carrot to the donkey. And a lot of us go the full journey without taking more than the odd nibble.

As a motivation, *lack* has got us this far, but it won't take us much further.

In a world where technology increasingly takes care of grassroots practicalities, there'll be a growing need to find meaning in our lives beyond a daily grind, because automation will be doing the grind for us. Ironically our survival will depend on shifting focus *away* from mere survival, and towards fulfillment.

But can we achieve this without our *curiosity?* A passive education deadens this essential aspect of our being and effectively neuters us. Without our curiosity compelling us to discover more; drawing us forward, fulfillment certainly *will* make us lazy.

So there we have it in a nutshell: ***we must do what it takes to preserve our children's curiosity.***

Our wider social values are not going to change overnight, but if we put our children in the driver's seat of their learning, we'll be taking a substantial step towards preserving their curiosity, and opening the way to a productive, fulfilling life for our future generations.

6

ORIGINAL

OR TYPICAL

How do we **rediscover**
our **uniqueness?**

The One and Only

Life without "normal" is hard to imagine. It's a line drawn in the sand – normal side equals good; other side equals *not* so good. *"The school says Josh is a perfectly normal boy!"* says one delighted parent to another. *"Phew... I was so worried he might not be...!"*

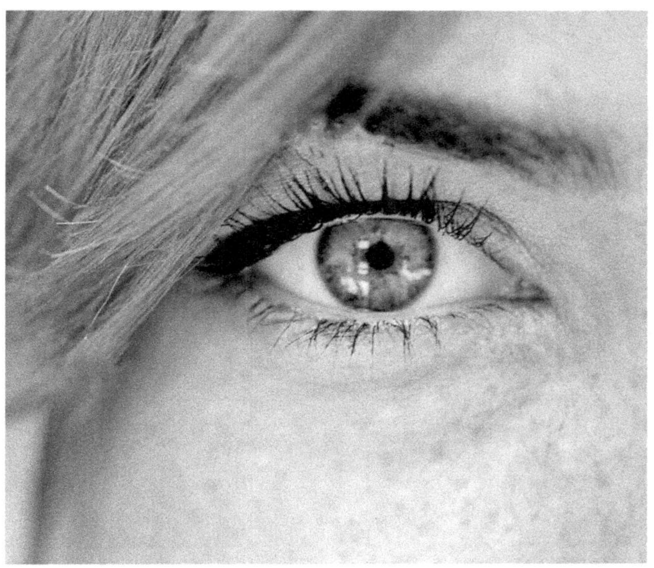

Though we're certainly influenced by the genes we've inherited, and by our environment, we're each of us unique beings from birth...

*... **One of a kind,*** in our hearts, bodies and minds.

Growing up in a social context, however, it's really tough to keep a grip on this uniqueness. When we're small, we just want to join in and play with the others, and we willingly push aside our unique inclinations so we'll be more readily accepted. So we'll be "normal".

For most of us, maintaining a seamless "normal" persona is an integral part of everyday life: scoping, assessing the reactions of the people we relate to, and moderating our behavior to stay in the normal zone.

Just the right mix. Familiar. Smart. Interest*ing* and interest*ed,* but not scarily so. And we've so absolutely mastered this program, that it runs pretty much automatically in the background while we get on with life. Talking, working, loving, playing. A constant self-auditing that edits out socially unacceptable behavior before it pops out and embarrasses us...

But what *good stuff* is it also editing out? What valuable aspects of our nature are we ditching so we can stay normal...?

It's not our fault. We get terribly mixed signals about being *unique* and yet *functional*, and we do our best. But we're going to have to look further below the surface.

Culture & Tradition

We often think of *culture* and *tradition* as closely-related concepts. We might say, *"it's a traditional way of doing things in my culture, so it's a part of my identity; part of who I am."* But it's now vitally important that we recognize the gulf of difference between the one, and the other. Between our *culture* and our *traditions*.

Culture makes us ***more...***

Culture helps a body of people to define and share a common group character. Each culture's strengths lie in its particular style of ***celebration:*** celebration of people, expression, nature, et cetera. With care and attention, an individual can relate to, and express, their cultural influences in a healthy way, without compromising their own uniqueness.

Tradition, however, makes us ***less...***

Tradition's primary purpose is to keep things the way they've always been, *because* they've always been that way – more an excuse than a reason! With its comforting familiarity, tradition brings a sense of solid ground, but prevents both the individual and their wider group from moving forward and growing.

Currently, traditional values define and dictate most of our important choices, like the way we learn, the job we do, and how we conduct our relationships. When we limit ourselves to prescribed options this way, we make the established social engine responsible for big chunks of our lives, and as a result, retain very little power over who we are and what we do.

Many of us feel like a little boat on a huge ocean – so much of what happens in our lives seems beyond our control. But we can gain a greater conscious grasp of the rudder if we re-assess the choices we made that brought us to where we are now.

What aspects of our lives are driven by traditional values...? What choices have we made as a result...? Where is the line between *culture*, and *tradition* in the things we do every day?

Often these choices are invisible to us because they are *the-way-things-are-done*-type-choices, and we originally made them with little thought about possible left-of-field alternatives: choices that are not on the traditional menu.

A sense of commitment to tradition is hard to shake. We might not always have a choice about how we *feel* about that, but we always have a choice as to how we *act.*

Conscious Choice

Some choices we're aware of making, and others, we're not. Often it's the choices we make *unconsciously* that hamstring our best efforts.

When the early steam locomotives ran the railways across nineteenth-century USA, free-ranging cattle would sometimes stray onto the tracks. The approaching train would blow its whistle, and the cow standing in the way would go into panic mode.

Of course, the cow *could've* just stepped off the track and let the train pass. The choice to do so was there. But not being the brightest of animals, the poor beast would often turn tail and run, straight along the track ahead of the train, eventually to be scooped bodily out of the way.

For obvious reasons – including dullness of intellect and fear – the cow couldn't appreciate the finer points of logic involved. It wasn't aware it had an alternative choice that could've saved it some anxiety and pain.

We humans are a lot smarter than the cow. But that doesn't mean we've got a handle on the full range of our choices. Those fiercely maintained traditions that revolve around the central aspects of our lives – relationships, work, self-expression, education – have us running for dear life along the tracks in front of the train!

It's bothersome to look beyond the choices we inherit from our social traditions, but our ability to define a wider range of choices *for ourselves* is a must-have if we want to re-access our uniqueness and really be ourselves.

The Flame Re-kindled

If we work hard at being unique, it's because we instinctively know that's where our really important answers lie. But, as always, if we don't fully understand the *questions,* our efforts will be misguided.

Uniqueness is not about how we appear to others. No kind of social status, hairstyle, clothing, tattoo, nor any other embellishment can compensate for the deep-down sense of unremarkableness so many of us feel, and strive to compensate for. Often it's the *least visibly* remarkable of us who are the most expressive of our uniqueness.

That feeling of unremarkableness is a result of wanting so deeply, for so long, to be accepted; of sidelining our unique inclinations, and of having long ago given up on ever taking the leap of faith required to reclaim them.

The only way to realistically deal with the feeling is to take that leap of faith, and to *keep* taking it, every minute of every day. But how do we know which way to leap...?

The number-one problem we have with defining who we are, comes from an assumption that we can use *existing definitions*. We try to take a generic idea and map it onto something unique; slotting ourselves into concrete categories like occupation, nationality, race, gender, style, habit. And while there's probably some small indication of our strengths in these things, the true basis of our being is far more subtle and diverse. What we're looking for won't be the same in any two people, so our search needs to be turned within.

Curiosity is the opener of the way to so many things,

including what makes each of us unique; the things that really make us tick. But an awful lot of us have been out of touch with this prime motivational force since childhood. We're not used to feeling it, listening to it and acting on what it says, and we have to get back into the habit that was so natural to us back then. It's quite manageable if we *pay attention.*

That's the starting point. To pay attention. To keep watch for the ripples of interest that announce curiosity's presence – and to pounce.

Watch... Catch.

We feel those first, subtle thrills and we act on them as quickly and as decisively as we can. We drop whatever we happen to be doing, and we run to find anything we think might in some way satisfy the curiosity. A conversation. A book. A google search. A phone call. A trip in the car. A rummage through the knick-knack drawer.

If it goes no particular place, well, that's all right. The momentum of curiosity leading us forward - even when short lived - is a worthwhile thing just for its own sake. But the more we follow the stirrings of interest, the more we get back into practice. The more we can find ourselves led further and further by the flow of our rediscovered curiosity.

The questions curiosity leads us to ask, are indicators. Whether it's clear to us or not, they show us – *remind* us – of what it is that defines us. Little things, quite often. Little glimpses of a bigger puzzle.

The thing to keep in mind is, there's more to these isolated little glimpses than we might think. They SEEM pointless and perhaps inconsequential, because they don't come with a built-in next step. We may well feel disappointed, expecting inspiration to come fully assembled and planned-out to its conclusion, but that's generally not the nature of the inspiration that curiosity brings. We have to take it

one... step... at... a... time.

When we've taken the first step, perhaps the next step will be suggested by something in the results of the first; or in the place we find ourselves brought to.

When we get into the swing of things a bit, we might start to see a pattern in our bursts of curiosity: the ***particular questions we have for the world***. It's those questions that we need to take up and run with and gradually bring into focus. The more we *clarify* those questions, the more we'll understand about ourselves and the unique perspective that defines us.

It's a kind of filtering down process – like when we

pan in a river for gold, there's a bunch of sand and stones in the pan along with any gold that's there, which we gradually swill and wash away to expose the good stuff.

But even when we've ditched all the sand and stones, all that glitters is not gold – as that old saying goes. Then again, it's fairly easy to tell what's real and what's not.

True gold is stuff we're happy to do for its own sake, without need of any other reward – financial or otherwise – if it comes down to it. It nourishes us in a way that transcends our "normal" appetites like comfort and convenience. We'll even choose an uncertain future if it means we can maintain that real nourishment.

And the fool's gold is also easy to spot, because it makes us weary. It makes us turn to comfort things like food and pretty things and social status, to compensate for the drudgery.

"Normal" life can get so horribly busy. Slowly bringing simplicity into our lifestyle – dropping away the things that make us weary; the excess things we have that demand constant attention and regular payments – really helps us narrow the focus to the important stuff. A big house that we have to work hard to pay for might be an asset socially, but is it making us weary? Are we in *working-to-survive-and-surviving-to-work* mode ?

Then there's the "useful" trap. We at last pinpoint an activity that truly nourishes us, and then put the squeeze on it by demanding it pay its way: *how will this earn me a living,* or *what practical uses can I put this to?* Concrete goals certainly allow us to achieve and to be productive, but they can damage our perception of our uniqueness and keep it beyond reach. We have to stay flexible. Always.

Lastly, uniqueness is not something we can settle into and find a complacent comfort in. It must be maintained like a garden and allowed to constantly grow; as must our greater sense of who we are.

It's something that needs to be consciously listened for, taken notice of, and nurtured.

Photo by LIYA TSUJI

DEREK W PEARSON is at various times a tutor for film and television studies, a writer, musician, filmmaker, digital artist and writer of course material for multimedia studies.

The son of two unconventionally-minded teachers, his everyday life has always been chock-full of creativity and change. He was born in North-Island New Zealand, and lives between his native country and Japan.

His current full-time focus is the After AI project, along with the development of a Non-Curricular Active Learning system.

Full bio at www.afterai-project.com

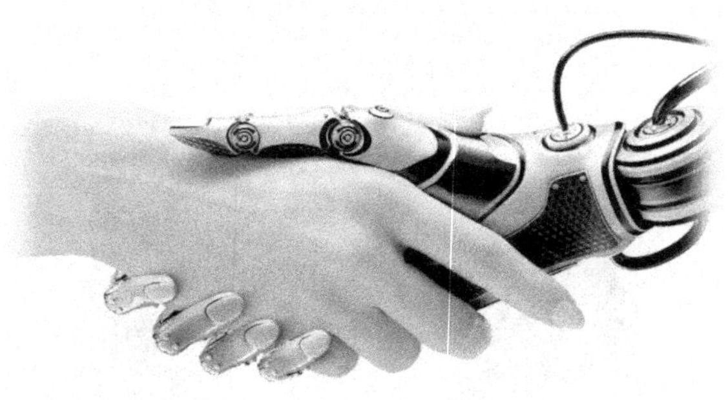

If you like the book, please consider donating!

(details at www.afterai-project.com)

DETAILED CONTENTS LIST

NOTES
&
REFERENCES

References

2   Ralph Jennings, Forbes.com, May 14, 2018. 'Why Unmanned Stores Are About To Take Off In China's Retail Market', https://www.forbes.com/sites/ralphjennings/2018 /05/14/why-china-is-uniquely-well-placed-to-develop-fully-automated-retail-stores/#4fe079b22aea

3   Sophie Curtis, Mirror, 27 March 2017. 'Bricklaying robots set to replace human builders on hundreds of UK construction sites', https://www.mirror.co.uk/tech/bricklaying-robots-set-replace-thousands-10107529

4   Ian Tucker, The Guardian, 20 May 2018. 'Autonomous car innovations: from jam busters to cures for queasiness', https://www.theguardian.com/technology/2018/ may/20/the-five-autonomous-car-innovations

5   Andrew J. Hawkins, The Verge, June 28, 2018. 'America's largest supermarket chain is launching a fully driverless delivery service', https://www.theverge.com/2018/6/28/17509856/ kroger-nuro-self-driving-car-delivery-partnership

6   Magdalena Osumi, Japan Times, January 18, 2018. 'Toto hopes to clean up with new self-cleaning toilets',

https://www.japantimes.co.jp/news/2018/01/18/nati
onal/toto-hopes-clean-new-self-cleaning-
toilets/#.W0mwQDkyV2E

7   A Cheong; MWS Lau; E Foo; J Hedley; Ju Wen Bo,
     Science Direct, Volume 49, Issue 21, 2016, pages
     681-686, 'Development of a Robotic Waiter System'
     (includes external references),
     https://www.sciencedirect.com/science/article/pii/S
     2405896316322911

8   Sayuri Daimon, Japan Times, September 9, 2015.
     'Will AI become a threat to future white-collar
     workers?',
     https://www.japantimes.co.jp/news/2015/09/09/bus
     iness/will-ai-become-a-threat-to-future-white-
     collar-workers/#.W0m1FTkyV2E

9   Emily Mullin, April 11, 2018, MIT technology
     review, "FDA approves first AI-powered
     diagnostic that doesn't need a doctors help",
     https://www.technologyreview.com/the-
     download/610853/fda-approves-first-ai-
     powered-diagnostic-that-doesnt-need-a-
     doctors-help/

10   i.   Kevin Kelleher, Time Magazine online,
                March 1 2017, 'How Artificial Intelligence
                Is Quietly Changing How You Shop
                Online',
                http://time.com/4685420/artificial-
                intelligence-online-shopping-retail-ai/
           ii. Anne Neal, RIS News, January 10, 2018. '6
                Ways Retail Technology Is Changing the

Future of Online Shopping',
https://risnews.com/6-ways-retail-technology-changing-future-online-shopping

11   Statista (no author credit; no date): 'Online-Shopping and E-Commerce worldwide: Statistics & Facts',
https://www.statista.com/topics/871/online-shopping/

15   (No author credit) Carewatch UK, 9 October (2017?). 'Top Personality Traits of a Carer',
https://www.carewatch.co.uk/blog/personality-traits-of-a-carer/15117/

17   i.   David Doody, GreenBiz, March 13 2014. '9 technologies that promise to clean up the planet',
https://www.greenbiz.com/blog/2014/03/13/can-clean-tech-save-the-world

         ii.   Tricia Escobedo, CNN, May 11 2017. '5 cool inventions that could save the planet',
https://edition.cnn.com/2017/05/11/tech/ecosolutions-5-ways-tech/index.html

22   Amit Chowdry, Forbes.com, September 18, 2018, "Artificial Intelligence To Create 58 Million New Jobs By 2022, Says Report",

https://www.forbes.com/sites/amitchowdhry/201
8/09/18/artificial-intelligence-to-create-58-
million-new-jobs-by-2022-says-
report/#19eeb8bd4d4b

23   (No author credit), Gallup.com, January 2018,
      "Optimism and Anxiety: Views on the Impact of
      Artificial Intelligence and Higher Education's
      Response", based on a survey conducted in 2017
      by Gallup and Northeastern University,
      https://news.gallup.com/reports/226475/gallup-
      northeastern-university-artificial-intelligence-
      report-2018.aspx#aspnetForm

24   Nick Butler, Financial Times, September 17, 2018,
      "Why the future of electric cars lies in China",
      https://www.ft.com/content/1c31817e-b5a4-
      11e8-b3ef-799c8613f4a1

www.ingramcontent.com/pod-product-compliance
Lightning Source LLC
Chambersburg PA
CBHW050957050726
47592CB00007B/2604